I have hidden your word in my heart,
that I might not sin against you.
—Psalm 119:11, NLT

For my family (past and present), friends, former colleagues and the new friends I will meet as I share some of my life's stories to bring your life's journey closer to God. I thank God for the opportunity to share my life stories in order to bring comfort to everyone reading my reflections and that they will find comfort in Him.

Blessed be the God and Father of our Lord Jesus
Christ, the Father of mercies and God of all
comfort, who comforts us in all our affliction
so that we will be able to comfort those who
are in any affliction with the comfort with
which we ourselves are comforted by God.
—2 Corinthians 1:3–4, NASB

Contents

REFLECTING SECTION

My Beginning Story 11

My Day of Salvation...14

Daddy's Lunch Bucket 16

Paydays Growing Up 18

My Piano Playing—My PaPaw Morris 20

The Garden Chair—My Dad..22

The Miscarriage—My Stepdaughter, Theresa 24

The Candy Bar...26

Fruit Trees—My Uncle Woody..28

My MaMaw Morris' Aprons..30

My MaMaw Morris' Journey to Heaven 32

LIVING SECTION

Turning Seventy—Seven Decades 37

The Rape 40

Hurricane Agnes, 1972...44

The Man on the Sidewalk 47

Alphabet—My Daughter, Beverly 49

The Cul-de-sac...51

Outsourcing..53

Too Quick to Judge—Finding Fault in Others 55

Our Aquarium 57

Challenges...59

Alaska—God's Creation Untouched by Man.......................61

Armor of God—My Granddaughter, Addie 62
Journey to Salvation—My Cousin Becky 64
Born of the Spirit—My Grandson, William 66

Trusting Section

End of High School—A New Journey....................................71
Sarah's Affliction and Strength..73
Obedience to God..75
Vultures..77
In God's Time 79
Family 81
Trusting God and His Spiritual Gifts—My
Daughter, Beverly..84
Trusting God Throughout Life's Tragedies—My
MaMaw Hall..86
A Few of Life's Choices..88
Be Aware of Idols 90

reflecting...

My Beginning Story

Portions Told to Me by My Mom, Dad, and Aunt Jenny

I was born at 3:15 a.m. to Paul William Hall and Norma May Morris Hall, on March 4, 1949, at the head of the holler in Keyrock, West Virginia, in a log cabin with no indoor plumbing or electricity. My Dad worked in the coal mines, and my Mom stayed at home and kept house and my older sister who was born in 1946.

Those present were my Mom's two midwives; my sister, Carolyn; my Aunt Jenny (Mom's sister), who was fifteen who came to help Mom before my birth. My Dad was at work. I was never told how he found out I was being born and to come home and bring the doctor, Dr. Wilkerson, and his wife, who was a nurse.

It was a very snowy night. Mom always told me I came into this world like a lion and would go out like a lamb. When I was born, my Mom's midwives informed my Mom that I was born with a veil on my face, and that if it weren't removed quickly, I would have died. They also told my Mom that the veil was a sign I would be beautiful, smart, see the future, have a special spirit, and bring joy to the world. When I got older, I learned this was the amniotic sac or a portion thereof. These are rare types of births. So, I was blessed from the moment I was born. My MaMaw Hall always told me I had special powers and would be able to predict the future. My family always talked about this and believed it. As a matter of fact, it was so well known throughout my family that if I had a "feeling," everyone would adhere to it.

I remember at times it seemed to be a burden, and I always didn't share my feelings but most of the time I did. My cousins still remember the veil story and listen to me. When I was younger, I remember my Mom, my aunts, and grandparents would always introduce me and add, "Linda was born with a veil on her face." They would look at me with amazement. I will confess, it always made me feel special, and I have continued to share this with my children and grandchildren. I used to laugh once people were told what the veil meant, I would joke and say that the beautiful part is true. I am thankful that my Mom had such knowledgeable midwives that removed the veil. *I just want to emphasize that my family never believed in spirits outside the Holy Spirit.*

> But if you are led by the Spirit, you are not under the Law. Now the deeds of the flesh are evident, which are: immorality, impurity, sensuality, idolatry, sorcery, enmities, strife, jealousy, outbursts of anger, disputes, dissensions, factions, envying, drunkenness, carousing, and things like these, of which I forewarn you, just as I have forewarned you, that those who practice such things will not inherit the kingdom of God. But the fruit of the Spirit is love, joy, peace, patience, kindness, goodness, faithfulness, gentleness, self-control; against such things there is no law. (Galatians 5:18–23, NASB)

My Mom and family always believed God had chosen me from the beginning for His ministry. I was saved at age nine, and I have shared that story later on in this book.

My Mom told me that the doctor arrived after my birth as he got stuck in the snow, and Daddy pulled or dug him out. Once the doctor arrived, my Mom had a vein burst in her leg, and she told me blood shot out everywhere. Dr. Wilkerson told her I was doing fine and that he arrived there in time to take care of her—another blessing on my birthday. Later in my life, she had to have surgery on her veins.

My Aunt Jenny named me and was always proud of this. Mom gave her the honor since she had come and helped her before I was born. Children were not named prior to birth as they had no means to know if the baby was a girl or boy. Therefore, naming took place at or shortly after birth. Aunt Jenny named me from a song, playing on the radio, "Linda Lou." I always joked with Aunt Jenny and my Mom saying that I was glad "John Henry" wasn't playing. It seemed they always laughed at that joke, which was always told after I was introduced, retelling the veil and the naming accounts. I guess those stories broke the ice and took the focus off the veil.

My Mom could not breastfeed me, so my formula was milk with Karo Syrup. My Mom told me she did supplement with SMA formula at times. She would purchase it at the Coal Company Store. She shared this with me when I had my first child, and the doctor put her on SMA. I remember thinking it did me no harm, so it would be safe for my daughter. SMA is still on the market with over ninety years of being in business.

All in all, I am so thankful for being born in Keyrock, West Virginia, surrounded by wonderful people, especially my parents. God allowed me to be born in a place that could not have been better in which to begin my life or to grow up.

> The Lord gave me this message; I knew you
> before I formed you in your mother's womb.
> —Jeremiah 1:4–5, NLT

> Are not two sparrows sold for a cent? And
> yet not one of them will fall to the ground
> apart from your Father. But the very hairs of
> your head are all numbered. So do not fear;
> you are more valuable than many sparrows.
> —Matthew 10:29–31, NASB

My Day of Salvation

I was fortunate to be able to walk to church from my home when growing up. This gave me the opportunity to go to all church services and actively participate in all youth activities.

We moved to this home when I was four, and Mom started taking us to Cook Memorial Baptist Church shortly after we moved. My brother was born here and was in that church at six weeks old. One can see how important this place was for us. We lived in a small town in West Virginia but one full of love and great people.

When I was nine, one Sunday night at church, our pastor, Reverend McCoy, had a great sermon; and I felt the calling of God to turn my life over to Him. However, when the invitation was given, I did not respond to His call. As we were leaving the church, I hung back to be the last to leave and shake my pastor's hand. When I got to Rev. McCoy to shake his hand, I started crying, and as he reached for my hand, I said, "I want to be a Christian." He told me to go up to the front of the church and wait for him. I did without hesitation. My Mom was looking for me, and he brought her up front to where I was sitting. She probably thought I was in trouble. He told her what had happened. He read me a few verses, prayed with me, and welcomed me to one of the saved. I remember this like it was yesterday. He scheduled my baptism date. I was happy, and my Mom was happier.

When it came to my baptism, I remember when I was immersed and went under the water I felt as if I were floating away. Even though it was a moment, my life changed forever. I came up happy, crying, and my life was changed. I was sealed, my name written in the book of life, and I would spend eternity in heaven with Jesus. I still live for Him today. I received the Holy Spirit at this baptism.

I never forgot the feeling of being immersed. However, a few years later I wanted that feeling again. When my brother got saved, I asked to be baptized again with him. They let me as a rededication to God in submission to full-time Christian service. When I was immersed that time, I did not "feel" the floating sensation as before, and when I came up out of the water, I realized I didn't need the second baptism. It was great being with my brother and rededicating my life, but my salvation baptism was the seal of my salvation. This is the first time I shared my second baptism.

> Peter replied, "each of you must repent
> of your sins and turn to God and be
> baptized in the name of Jesus Christ for
> the forgiveness of your sins. Then you
> will receive the gift of the Holy Spirit.
> —Acts 2:38, NLT

Daddy's Lunch Bucket

I was born in 1949 on a snowy night at the head of holler called Keyrock, West Virginia. I had a sister three years older and did not get a brother until I was six. My Dad worked in the coal mines when we lived in Keyrock until I was four when he got a job with the power company, and we moved to Pineville, West Virginia—a few miles from Keyrock from the head of a holler to the mouth of the holler called Bear Hole.

I had six years of being the baby and Daddy's little girl. When Dad would come home from work, he always saved me something from his lunch. I can remember running down the path to carry his lunch bucket to the house. When I was almost eight, and my baby brother was growing up, one day, I met Daddy; and he did not give me his lunch bucket. He carried it to the house and handed it to my brother as he had saved his "something" for him as I was no longer the baby. I'll never forget the hurt, and that was a huge first step in me growing up. I did not resent my brother, but I remember being upset—but I never told Dad and Mom this until I grew up and became an adult. Dad didn't do this because he didn't love me or loved my brother more, but in his eyes, I had outgrown the bucket treats.

I have always tried to treat my children equal in all things. I am not sure if this was good or bad, but these actions came from me never wanting my kids to feel the same pain I had. I am still doing this "fairness" activity today.

God also treats us like this when we are saved, we should come to God as children, eager to learn, and start growing and maturing in our walk with Him. If we stay as a child and not study His word, pray and talk with Him as well as mature in our walk, we will miss our greatest blessings. As my Dad "made me grow up" that day, God lets us go through trials and storms, so we learn to depend on Him and mature. If we let Him take us through a storm, we will always come out with wisdom, testimony, and a dependence on our Heavenly Father, which is His desire. Thank you, God, for the trials—thank you, Daddy, for encouraging me to grow!

> You have been believers so long now that you
> ought to be teaching others. Instead you need
> someone to teach you again the basic things
> about God's Word. You are like babies who
> need milk and cannot eat solid food. For
> someone who lives on milk is still an infant
> and doesn't know how to do what is right.
> Solid food is for those who are mature, who
> through training have the skill to recognize
> the difference between right and wrong.
> —Hebrews 5:12–14, NLT

> So let us stop going over the basic teachings
> about Christ again and again. Let us go
> on instead and become mature in our
> understanding. Surely, we don't need to start
> again with the fundamental importance
> of repenting from evil deeds and placing
> our faith in God. You don't need further
> instructions about baptism, the laying on
> of hands, the resurrection of the dead and
> eternal judgement. And so, God willing, we
> will move forward to further understanding.
> —Hebrews 6:1–3, NLT

Paydays Growing Up

I was born and raised in Wyoming County, West Virginia. Born in Keyrock and lived there until I was four years old, we moved to a house in Pineville, West Virginia.

During the last year of our living at Keyrock, Dad got a job with the Appalachian Power Company; and we were able to move to Pineville. Dad no longer had to work in the coal mines.

When my sister, brother, and I got a little older, every payday, Mom would pick us up something special—clothes and shoes—and lay them on our bed. When we came home from school, and Mom had been to the store, even though my Dad did not make a lot of money, Mom always managed to make us feel special.

Reflecting on this story, it warms my heart that the little things that happened during my childhood are memorable. I can close my eyes and see the purple plaid skirt and purple sweater on my bed after school on one payday.

I always strived to make memories like this for our children as they grew up just to show them and teach them the importance of giving and receiving as my Mom always gave when there was not much to give—warms my heart as if it were yesterday.

Children, obey your parents in the Lord, for
this is right. HONOR YOUR FATHER AND
MOTHER (which is the first commandment

with a promise), SO THAT IT MAY BE
WELL WITH YOU, AND THAT YOU
MAY LIVE LONG ON THE EARTH.
—Ephesians 6:2–3, NASB

My Piano Playing—
My PaPaw Morris

One of the many blessings of my childhood was the great relationship I had with my grandparents—MaMaw and PaPaw Morris and MaMaw Hall. PaPaw Hall passed away when I was four. This story I would like to share about PaPaw Morris.

We would visit PaPaw and MaMaw Morris, and no matter when we visited, we would go to church—all riding on kitchen chairs in the back of his truck.

My PaPaw played the piano like none other. He, at one time in his life, played for silent movies but spent his time now playing for his family and church.

I took piano lessons for several years but have never been able to master it like him or my Mom, both played by ear. "Choppy" was the best way to describe my playing as I was learning.

One Sunday, we were visiting them and went to church. My PaPaw stood up in church and announced to the congregation that they had a treat in store for them as I was going to play for the church that day and that I didn't play like him but played the piano by reading music and not by ear. I felt so honored that my PaPaw was so proud of me. That morning, I played all the congregational hymns, the offertory, and the closing hymn as everyone was leaving the church.

Sometime later, I was reflecting on this day and that was when I realized what agony I had put that church through that morning. Nonetheless, everyone in that church sang to my choppy missing notes playing and even congratulated me afterwards. My PaPaw spoke only truth that day as I "did not play like him" and never would.

This entire act just showed how wonderful a man my PaPaw was—he offered me encouragement probably when I needed it most, and the wonderful people of that church "suffered" through my playing, and no one—the people I did not know nor the ones I did like my Mom, sister, MaMaw, aunts, nor cousins—said anything negative. I remember all of them telling me that Sunday how good I was.

I wonder if people would be so kind today as the world laughs at anything that is not perfect—singing, music, weight, etc.

I also know that his encouragement made me go on with my piano playing. I learned to play better and have served as a church pianist in several churches. This serving of God might had been stifled if that day PaPaw gave me a chance had turned out different.

Thank you, PaPaw, and thanks to all those wonderful strangers and my family who supported a scared little girl.

> Remind them to be subject to rulers, to
> authorities, to be obedient, to be ready for every
> good deed, to malign no one, to be peaceable,
> gentle, showing every consideration for all men.
> —Titus 3:1–2, NASB

The Garden Chair—My Dad

Every growing season, we would always count on Dad and Mom's bountiful harvest. From that, we would get fresh vegetables each year that we canned and froze for the winter months. Life was all so in place and good.

Then Dad and Mom aged, and with that, the gardens that we loved also ceased. We would go and plant gardens and tend to them since they enjoyed the gardens so much but never did our gardens produce the harvests of my parents.

During that time, Dad still loved to go to the garden, and he carried to the garden an old metal folding chair and would sit for hours, watching the garden at its edge under the trees. We often thought that his presence there helped the garden to grow.

In 2000, Dad was taken to his heavenly home. We would visit the garden after his death and sit by the chair he sat in for so long and feel his presence still watching over the garden. The chair still sits there today.

In life, we do so many things, and like Dad, watching over the garden our Heavenly Father watches over us to help us grow and harvest souls for His Kingdom.

> I will greatly rejoice in the Lord, my soul
> will exult in my God, for He hath clothed
> me with garments of salvation...for as the
> earth brings forth its sprouts, and as a garden

causeth the things sown in it to spring up; so
the Lord God will cause righteousness and
praise to spring up before all the nations.
—Isaiah 61:10–11, NASB

The Miscarriage—
My Stepdaughter, Theresa

Things occur in life that we will never understand! Almost twenty years ago, my stepdaughter was married and became pregnant at the same time as my two nieces. All babies were due around the same time. My two nieces had successful births, but my stepdaughter had a miscarriage. I can only imagine how difficult it was for her to watch her cousins deliver healthy babies and see them get older each year.

After her miscarriage, she discovered her husband was involved in sinful/illegal behavior, which resulted in their divorce. After the divorce, she started back to grad school—got her masters and her PhD. She now has a successful career in helping others doing medical research. Without her going through these storms, she would not be where she is today.

Even though she will never get over her loss, she should always be thankful for the new door, which God opened for her.

We always need to reflect on our "storms" and what God wants us to learn from them. I tell her and I tell myself, do not dwell on all the negatives but rejoice in the new path. This can only happen once you turn everything over to God and let Him help you succeed in your new walk.

Thank you, Jesus, for everything!!

> For God called you to do good, even if it means
> suffering, just as Christ suffered for you. He is
> your example, and you must follow in His steps.

He never sinned, nor ever deceived anyone. He did not retaliate when he was insulted nor threaten revenge when he suffered. He left his case in the hands of God, who always judges fairly. He personally carried our sins in his body and on the cross so that we can be dead to sin and live for what is right. By his wounds you are healed. Once you were like sheep who wandered away. But now you have turned to your Shepherd, the Guardian of your souls.

—1 Peter 2:21–25, NLT

The Candy Bar

My brother had a heart attack in 2009. I was working in Minneapolis, and he lives near Dallas. After his attack, his lungs filled with blood clots. Instead of flying home, I flew to Dallas to work from there the next week and to see him. I am thankful to God for allowing me to be that flexible in my job and most of all Him healing my brother.

I'll never forget the worried look on his wife and son's faces. My brother got to come home, and I got to spend real quality time with him, his wife, and my nephew. What started as worry ended as a blessing! Thank you, Jesus.

During the week, I went to the store, and I picked up a candy bar and brought it home to my nephew. At the end of this week, I flew home. A long time after I was talking with my brother, he mentioned that my nephew still had not eaten the candy bar as it was a reminder of me and that week. I felt overwhelmed.

It also reminded me of how we can always remember God and His love for us. Just look outside—the sky, sun, moon, stars, trees, grass, birds, and other animals—everything comes from God, and we are made in His image. What a privilege. As my nephew kept that candy bar, we should keep God's Word the Bible near us and in our hearts. Not only to remember but to grow closer to God each day.

Thanks to my nephew for being a kind and caring person, but most of all for being you and teaching us the importance of remembering.

Your eternal word, O Lord, stands firm in Heaven. Your faithfulness extends to every generation, as enduring as the earth you created. Your regulations remain true to this day, for everything serves your plans. If your instructions hadn't sustained me with joy, I would have died in my misery. I will never forget your commandments, for by them you give me life. I am yours; rescue me! For I have worked hard at obeying your commandments. Though the wicked hide along the way to kill me, I will quietly keep my mind on your laws. Even perfection has its limits, but your commands have no limit!
—Psalm 119:89–96, NLT

Fruit Trees—My Uncle Woody

Throughout our life we do things, go places, and really leave our mark wherever we go. None was so active doing this as my Uncle Woodrow Ramsey (we call him Uncle Woody). Uncle Woody loved the land and especially the mountains of West Virginia. Uncle Woody dug ginseng and sold it to earn some money. While in the woods, "senging," he took fruit with him to eat—apples, peaches, cherries, etc. He would rest and eat his fruit. After he ate the fruit, he would find a place and plant the seed so a new tree would grow. He watched many trees grow and provided more fruit to eat. The hills he walked in are full of these trees.

He also planted chestnut trees. He visited my Mom and Dad when they were living in Virginia, and he brought them a small chestnut tree. My Dad and Uncle Woody planted it, and today, it is a huge beautiful shade tree at the end of my parents' garden. They enjoyed the shade of the tree many times. Uncle Woody left a legacy of trees for people to enjoy. He also preached God's Word, and all five of his children are Christians. This causes me to wonder and ask, *What am I going to leave?* Uncle Woody left trees to benefit those he never knew and taught the love of God to many who have passed it on. His story lives on from generation to generation.

We all need to leave timeless godly treasures. Our only purpose is to serve God, protect His land, and show others the way of the cross by our loving witness.

What is your legacy?

> Do not be deceived, God is not mocked; for
> whatever a man sows, this he will also reap.
> —Galatians 6:7, NASB

My MaMaw Morris' Aprons

There are many good memories of my childhood especially those with my PaPaw and MaMaw Morris. I thank God often for my upbringing and how fortunate I was to have grandparents who loved me as their own.

My MaMaw Morris wore aprons every day, except on Sunday when she went to church. These aprons went around her neck and covered her whole front and sides of the dress she wore. I never remember her wearing pants. My mother made most of her aprons.

She wore these to protect her clothes and to help her throughout the day. They had pockets for her to carry things, she would wipe her hands on them as she lifted them up like a towel. She would string beans on her lap, using the apron, to hold the beans and roll it up to carry outside to throw away the strings. She would use her apron as a pot holder as she moved iron skillets on her coal cooking stove. When she aged, even though she didn't do a lot of things, she still wore the aprons; and my Mom made new ones for her until MaMaw died. I wish I had one of them.

As I think about the apron, I often reflect on the protection and many uses they gave her. It protected her clothing, it allowed her to carry items she needed, and it had so many different uses.

When reflecting on this. I likened it to God's armor. We are to put on the armor of God daily to keep us in our walk. So as the apron memories comfort me, knowing that I have God's armor to protect me is even more comforting. Make sure you put on God's armor each and every day.

- Helmet—Salvation is our helmet
- Shield—Shield of faith to stop the fiery arrows of the devil
- Sword—Sword of spirit, the Word of God
- Body Armor—God's righteousness
- Belt—Belt of truth
- Shoes—Put on the peace that comes from good news to be fully prepared (note: Roman soldiers' sandals had a long spike at the heel of their shoe, which allowed them to plant their feet firmly in the ground).

Pray in the spirit at all times and on every occasion.

> Therefore, put on every piece of God's armor
> so you will be able to resist the enemy in the
> time of evil. Then after the battle you will still
> be standing firm. Stand your ground, putting
> on the belt of truth and the body armor of
> God's righteousness. For shoes, put on the
> peace that comes from the Good News so
> that you will be fully prepared. In addition
> to all of these, hold up the shield of faith
> to stop the fiery arrows of the devil. Put on
> salvation as your helmet, and take the sword
> of the Spirit, which is the word of God.
> —Ephesians 6:13–17, NLT

My MaMaw Morris' Journey to Heaven

My MaMaw Morris was a wonderful woman who loved her family dearly. I remember so many wonderful things about her and even a few that got me upset at times. As I look back on the aggravations, I am pleased because those difficult feelings show how close we were. A relationship only grows through its ups and downs.

At the end of her life, she was sick for several months. I lived in Virginia near my parents. It seemed every weekend or so we would get the call to come visit her to say our goodbyes. Mom and I would immediately pack and hit the road for the four-plus-hour drive to West Virginia to say our goodbyes. I was working during this time and would drop everything and take my Mom to see her Mom, my MaMaw. I remember telling my work that I was leaving, not asking permission. I could always find another job, but the right thing was to take Mom. They never said anything negative about my leaving and supported me during this time.

On the final trip to see MaMaw, my Mom and I walked into her hospital room, and she was so very ill. There was an odor like none other. All my aunts, uncles, and many cousins were there. After a visit, Mom and I went and checked into our motel room and got some lunch. On the way back to the hospital, I stopped at a store and got Clorox disinfectant spray and an odor remover for MaMaw's room. She was always such a clean person, and I knew she would not want to smell this way. I also got her some Chapstick as her lips were so dry and I knew that must be uncomfortable for her.

When we got back to the hospital, we went into her room, and I sprayed the Clorox in her garbage cans and around the room to get rid of the smell. I also put Chapstick on her dry lips. I knew the smell was the smell of death, and no Clorox could make it go away completely. While we were in the room, a nurse came in and asked us to leave so they could clean MaMaw and her room. We left and went to the waiting room down the hall with the rest of our family.

After a while, I looked down the hall and saw the nurse leave MaMaw's room. I left the crowd and walked alone to her room and sat down. When I entered the room, it was so clean and bright. My Aunt Gloria came in and sat beside me, and we discussed what a great job the nurses had done cleaning—no smell, and it was very bright.

Aunt Gloria and I sat there alone. At some point, we started counting MaMaw's breaths per minute. They got slower and less often—; one time, only seven breaths per minute. We sat quietly for several minutes. Then all at once, my MaMaw raised her hand and breathed loudly—. We immediately said in unison—, "When I take my last fleeting breath." We sat there.

Then Gloria said, "I guess I'd better tell the nurse that she has died." She got the nurse, they asked us to step out, and then they pronounced her dead.

Gloria and I looked at each other and said, "The brightness were the angels coming to carry her home." We were calm and thanked God for letting us be present.

I went to the waiting room and told everyone MaMaw had died and then the peace was over. Everyone started to cry and scream. I remember trying to tell everyone how peaceful it was and then heard comments as to why didn't Gloria and I come and get them. We weren't supposed to. God chose us to see MaMaw's departure, and for that, we are always thankful.

This story came to mind this morning as I was reading my morning devotions, Luke 24. As Jesus ascended into heaven, so will we if we die with Christ. That is what we witnessed with my MaMaw and Gloria's Mom. Are you heaven bound?

And He led them out as far as Bethany, and He lifted up his hands and blessed them. While He was blessing them; He parted from them and was carried up into Heaven. And they, after worshiping Him, returned to Jerusalem with great joy and were continually in the temple praising God.

—Luke 24:50–53, NASB

living...

Turning Seventy—Seven Decades

(God's Perfect Number)

On March 4, 2019, I turned seventy years old. As I reflect, I thank God for the life he gave me. I also thank God for the people He let me share it with—to name a few, a very few.

First decade (1949–1959). I was born at home on March 4, 1949. My Mom's midwives were there. My Aunt Jenny named me. My Dad left the mines for the power company, which then we moved from a head of holler to a mouth of a holler. A lot of other things happened—my brother's birth; my PaPaw Hall's death; my Mom for taking us to church; my friends/neighbors, Diana, Donna, Debbie, and their moms, Hazel, Millie, and Hilda; and my salvation at age nine. It was a great first decade.

Second decade (1960–1969). My parents, my siblings, Carolyn and Billy, 4–H club, church, BYF, school dances, marching band, walking to town, piano lessons, singing, our neighbor, Sadie, my grandparents, uncles, aunts, and cousins. When I moved to Virginia, I met my new lifelong friend, Lynne. I had my first job and first car. I graduated from high school. President Kennedy was assassinated. My life was so full and rich with blessings.

Third decade (1970–1979). New friends; jobs; bosses; starting the gospel group and leading *The New Disciples*; serving God; my rape; meeting my husband; getting married; my first child; my pastors; my Mom and Dad and my new nieces and nephew; losing my PaPaw Morris; Hurricane Agnes; and our first home.

Fourth decade (1980–1989). I was working on Capitol Hill for two congressmen; my second child; my stepchildren; our family beach vacations; Disney World; my jobs; all our blessings; our new house; Sarah's illness; God's watchful eye; marriage issues and marriage mends; and losing my MaMaw Morris and several aunts and uncles' deaths. My husband retired from the Air Force.

Fifth decade (1990–1999). Life continues. My children graduate school, and went on to college. I was close to my cousins. There were surgeries. My sister was ill. A new nephew was born. Member of school board; hurts and healings; served God; community gospel sing leader; travels, and great family times.

Sixth decade (2000–2009). My Dad died on September 20, 2000, and life was never the same. On September 11, 2001, the Twin Towers in New York were destroyed by terrorists. Children graduate college. Youngest daughter marries, and first granddaughter was born (2008). We sold Virginia home, lived with Mom for over a year, moved to North Carolina, and had new home and job. I traveled a lot, three and a half years in Minnesota. My mother moved in with us in February 2007 until she died on December 25, 2007. Life once again will never be the same. We moved into final home, and God has never left us/me. We had new friends and many blessings.

Seventh decade (2010–2019). We went to a new church, had a new grandson (2011), and had new job opportunities. I traveled to India and England with job; also traveled to Alaska with my daughters, granddaughter, my brother, and his family. I was closer to my brother again and a great relationship with my sister-in-law. I was looking for new place to worship. God is providing, and I am still depending on him. I retired on September 2017. I am looking forward to many more years of serving God. My brother-in-law, Lloyd, died March 16, 2019.

Future decades (2020–20??). I intend to live for God and continue to watch my children and grandchildren grow.

I have been crucified with Christ; and it
is no longer I who live, but Christ lives in
me; and the life which I now live in the
flesh I live by faith in the Son of God, who
loved me and gave himself up for me.
—Galatians 2:20, NASB

The Rape

I remember the night as if it were yesterday, and it happened over forty-five years ago.

This was a happy and active time in my life going about doing the Lord's work. My friends and I were in a gospel-singing group, and we traveled and sang all over the Washington DC metropolitan area in churches, coffee houses, street corners, and we even traveled to upstate New York once to sing. We decided that we would make a recording since everywhere we sang, people asked if we had a record. I was the leader of the group, and we had an adult manager that we loved and appreciated her time working with and supporting us.

I cannot even remember how we found the gospel recording studio in Maryland, but we did. We were introduced to one of the principles at the studio that was a man of God, I will call him "Terror." He could play the piano like none other and had made several records of his own. He started coming to our concerts and talked about recording the group. We were so excited.

I was single during this time and was praying daily for God to send me a man to spend the rest of my life with, working for Him. When I met the man from the recording studio, I thought that this must be the answer to my prayers. We dated a few times, and we even spoke of marriage and spending our lives going about doing the Lord's work. How perfect was this?

One night, he picked me up, and we were going to the recording studio to make some arrangements for the group's recording. On the way to the studio, he said he had to stop by his house to pick up some records he was reviewing. We stopped, went inside, and he played several songs on the piano and organ; and I was happy. He then told me he wanted me to hear one of the albums he was reviewing and took me into his room to listen. He started playing one of the gospel records, turned it up loud, and then threw me on the bed and raped me. When he finished, he threw me across the bed, yelled, and told me to get up. My clothes were not completely off, my underwear was at my ankles, I was humiliated, and I cried realizing surely, he was not a man of God. Then we left.

We got in the car, drove to the studio, he would not take me home—he acted as if nothing had happened. He even tried to be nice to me. He also threatened that if I told anyone, he would really hurt me and that no one would believe me anyway.

After the rape, I knew I must be examined by a doctor, and I called the next day for an emergency appointment. After the doctor examined me, he advised that I had been severely harmed and wanted details of what had happened. I told him of the rape. He asked if I wanted to press charges, I was scared and said no. One must remember that during this time, there was no such thing as "date rape." The doctor also scheduled me to have an antibiotic treatment for ten days. I stopped each day after work and received an injection. He also advised me to confide in someone that I trusted as I was going to need support.

The next day, "Terror" called and told me that he had called our singing group's manager and told her that we had been sleeping together and that she would not believe me if I told her of the rape. I immediately called my manager, told her what happened, and she said, "I understand, my husband and I slept together before we were married too." I could not believe my ears, she believed him and not me. I told my other friends, and they believed his story too. I was alone.

For if they fall, the one will lift up his fellow:
but woe to him that is alone when he falleth; for

he hath not another to help him up. (Eccles. 4:10)

My parents lived in another state, and I went home to visit them. I did not share with anyone else what had happened. When I returned to work, one of my coworkers told me that a man had called me several times and tried to get him to tell him where I had gone. I thanked my coworker for not letting him know where I was and confided in him my situation. He was so caring and comforting and told me that he would make sure I would not be harmed.

Then, "Terror" started calling me at work and told me that he was coming to my office. I worked at the Pentagon at the time, and since it was secure, I felt safe there. He said that he had to see me again and that he was going to cause trouble for me at the guard's desk if I did not see him. I told my coworker of these calls and he said we could have him arrested. I was horrified. Then "Terror" told me that he had found my car at my bus stop and advised that I would not be able to get it started. He said he would meet me there and cause a scene. I then agreed, to my coworker's disapproval, to go with him to my car. My coworker called the police and asked them to be at my car when I arrived.

The drive to my car seemed like an eternity, and I prayed all the way. On the ride to my car, he apologized for raping me, tried to touch my hand, which I pushed away, and told him I never wanted to see, hear, or even know about him ever again. When we reached my car, the tire was flat, and he had taken a piece off the engine so it would not start. He put air in my tire with a portable pump and put the piece back on my engine. A policeman was sitting near the car, and I thanked God for my coworker. The policeman got of his car and asked if I was all right. After I assured him I was, he told "Terror" never to contact me again. I knew the relationship with "Terror" was finally over, but now I had to deal with all the baggage that was left.

I tried to keep singing with the group, and one day after a concert, we all talked, and we decided that I would not sing with them again. The spirit had been quenched, and the devil had torn away our bond. I remember driving away with tears in my eyes but a burden off my back. I knew in order to continue in my walk with God that I would have to forgive them, even "Terror."

> For if you forgive others for their transgressions, your heavenly Father will also forgive you. (Matt. 6:14, NASB)

Life went on, I joined a different church and began a whole new mission with new brothers and sisters in Christ. A few years later, I was standing in line in a copy room at work, waiting for a copier, and this girl came up to me and said, "You know 'Terror,' don't you?" I felt nauseous. I asked how she knew, and she said, "He did to me what he did to you." We walked away and talked a long time. "Terror" had told her about what he had done. She told me that no one believed her either. We cried and prayed together. I never saw her again. I often thought of her as an angel.

I never told my friends and/or the manager how hurt I was that they thought I could sin that way. I still correspond with one of the group's members. One of these days, I intend to share with her this story, and maybe we can forgive each other for not being a true friend—me not telling her how hurt and angry I was, and her not trusting or believing in me.

> Confess your sins one to another, and
> pray one for another, that ye may be
> healed. The effectual fervent prayer of
> a righteous man accomplish much.
> —James 5:16, NASB

> Teaching them to observe all that I have
> commanded you: and, lo, I am with you
> always, even unto the end of the age. Amen.
> —Matthew 28:20, NASB

Hurricane Agnes, 1972

When you live inland, one never worries about hurricanes, some rain from them maybe, but no real damage. That all changed in June 1972. My sister, her husband, two young daughters, and an infant one-month old son lived in Woodbridge, Virginia. I also lived in Woodbridge in an apartment a few miles away.

The rain would never let up that day. My sister lived in a mobile home with a little stream behind it, so small, we used to say we could put our foot in it and would not get it wet. We were warned that massive flooding was coming to Woodbridge. As my brother-in-law watched the little stream behind their home get larger and rougher, he suggested my sister and the children come to my apartment. A few hours later, my brother-in-law came to my apartment and just shook his head, stating that the water was going into the door of the home. I had eighteen people that night in my one-bedroom apartment, people who were displaced by the flood. Woodbridge lost power and its water, but thanks be to God, we never lost power or water at my apartment complex.

The next morning, my brother-in-law went to check on their home, and it had been flooded to the top of the windows and then pulled off its foundation. Later, we learned that a culvert that ran under a railroad track, near their home, had gotten jammed with floating debris and stopped it up so the water could only rise. When the pressure of the water broke through the culvert, it was like that to a bathtub, letting the water out and the force of that pulled many

44

homes off their foundations. My sister's family and thirty other families lost their homes that day.

We retrieved as many clothes (all muddy) and brought them to my apartment. I washed and dried eighteen loads of clothes in one day, praising God that we never lost power or water at my apartment.

Months later, they moved to Fredericksburg, Virginia in a new home away from any streams. Since they lost their furniture, I decided to move in with them and gave them all I had to help them not having to replace them all. I personally enjoyed living with them and being around my nieces and nephew; we were all winners. We always praised God for bringing us through the storm and making it brighter on the other side. I am not sure my sister ever got over this trial, but she went on living and raised a beautiful family and now has grandchildren as they never lost their faith in God.

> For this reason I say to you, do not be worried about your life, as to what you will eat or what you will drink; nor for your body, as to what you will put on. Is not life more than food, and the body more than clothing? Look at the birds of the air, that they do not sow, nor reap nor gather into barns, and yet your heavenly Father feeds them. Are you not worth much more than they? And who of you by being worried can add a single hour to his life? And why are you worried about clothing? Observe how the lilies of the field grow; they do not toil nor do they spin, yet I say to you that not even Solomon in all his glory clothed himself like one of these. But if God so clothes the grass of the field, which is alive today and tomorrow is thrown into the furnace, will He not much more clothe you? You of little faith! Do not worry then, saying, 'What will we eat?' or 'What will we drink?' or 'What will we wear

for clothing?' For the Gentiles eagerly seek all these things; for your heavenly Father knows that you need all these things. But seek first His kingdom and His righteousness, and all these things will be added to you. "So do not worry about tomorrow; for tomorrow will care for itself. Each day has enough trouble of its own.

—Matthew 6:25–34, NASB

The Man on the Sidewalk

It was a typical busy workday, and I worked for a small law firm in a small town. Our motto was "nothing would get done if it weren't for the last minute." It was also a busy time of the year; Christmas was just around the corner and not enough time to do all the things that needed to be done.

I was the choir director at a church about twenty miles from my job, and we were preparing for the Christmas Cantata. I also had two young children that were in elementary school, a husband who commuted over fifty miles to and from work each day, a family that also demanded my time, school clubs, etc., and they needed my focus.

One Wednesday, during this season, I had to work until 6:30 p.m. and choir practice started at 7:30 p.m. I knew I was going to be late as I had to pick up my children and my husband, pick up my mother, and try to get everyone something to eat prior to going to practice. I left work in a hurry, jumped in my car, and rushed to do the Lord's work.

As I left work, I had to drive through a downtown community. As I came to this intersection, I noticed a man's hat had blown into the street and the man was standing on the sidewalk. I thought I am in too big of a hurry to stop for that hat, he can get it, so I drove around it and went on. As soon as I did, Matthew 25:40 came into my head:

> And the King shall answer and say unto them, Verily I say unto you, Inasmuch as ye have done it unto one of the least of these my brethren, ye have done it unto me.

I knew I might be late, but I had to go and help that man. I turned around and drove back (took about three to four minutes) and the hat was still in the middle of the street. I stopped my car, got out, picked up the hat, noticed it was new, and took it to the man who was still standing on the sidewalk.

When I got up to the man, he was shaking, and I handed him his hat and said, "I believe this is yours." He said, "Thank you," and had tears in his eyes. It was then that I noticed he was blind. He would not have been able to find his new hat. He thanked me again and again and just held onto my hands. And I cried.

When I left him, I got in my car and thanked God that His Word had sent me back to help that man. I got to choir practice on time, shared my testimony, and our practice was one of the best. By having learned Matthew 25:40 many years before, I was able to receive the blessing that God had in store for me.

We should never be so preoccupied in what we think is God's work that we fail to do the real work that we are put here to do.

> I have hidden your word in my heart,
> that I might not sin against you.
> —Psalm 119:11, NLT

Alphabet—My Daughter, Beverly

God made each one of us unique and like none other. A fact of this is our fingerprints and DNA are unique. When two people create children, even though the children are born of the same parents, they are not alike and are their own person.

Our firstborn would go to preschool and share with us everything about her day. Our second born would not share anything.

One day, when Beverly, our second born, was in preschool, I received her assessment, she was two and a half years old. When I read it, it showed she could count to one hundred and knew her entire alphabet. I remember how overwhelmed with joy I was but also wondered why she never shared this success.

On our way home, I asked her "Beverly, why didn't you tell us you knew the alphabet?" She immediately responded, "Doesn't everybody." This blew me away, and my Mom and I just smiled. I knew right then that she was going to be successful in life. She knew what she needed to know and learned it without fanfare! Her understanding of knowledge was matter-of-fact; learn and move on to learn more.

We can follow this example in our daily walk with God. One time, a minister said that when we fill up with food, we get full and are satisfied. In reading God's Word, we fill up but are never satisfied and want more and more of God's Word. As Beverly absorbed new things and is eager to learn more, we should study God's word eager to learn what His plans are for us. She is very successful in her career and her walk with God, still eager to learn, live and share.

> [Jesus speaking] What is the price of five
> sparrows—two copper coins? Yet God does
> not forget a single one of them. And the
> very hairs on your head are all numbered.
> So don't be afraid; you are more valuable to
> God than a whole flock of sparrows. God
> cares for us so much that He even knows
> the exact number of hairs on our heads.
> —Luke 12:6–7, NLT

In these verses, Jesus reminds us that God cares for every sparrow—but He cares for us even more.

The Cul-de-sac

As life goes on, our children grow up and begin lives of their own. No longer needing our daily guidance. Our hope as parents is that we prepared them for the future. The following poem was one that I wrote and gave to all families in our subdivision that lived in our cul-de-sac as the children were leaving one by one. I am sharing here what I think signifies that "life goes on" as everyone grows.

> The snow lays gently on the cul-de-sac
> Not a footprint or snowman—yes, the snow is
> intact.
> It is beautiful and smooth but also so quiet
> I gaze out my window and the memories flood
> back.
> I remember so many children that grew up
> playing here
> Tin can alley, hopscotch, biking—such cheer.
> But now they are gone, just the parents remain
> Their hair turning gray and their backs in pain.
> Eric was the first to leave the cul-de-sac team
> Then as each year passed, others left, too quick
> it did seem.
> Shannon, Sarah, Brian, and Kim each started
> life's race
> Leaving Beverly alone to finish with grace.

Now Beverly is gone, and the cul-de-sac is quiet
Just adults here now that turn their lights off
    early at night.
No more leaving the porch lights on to welcome
    them home
Yes, the cul-de-sac is empty and the parents alone.
I turn from the window with tears in my eyes
Too many memories and then I realize
Life will never again be the same in the cul-de-sac
We will only have memories and then try to relax.
But then I hear noise, laughter and cheer,
It's the Spoons' grandchildren out and about
Building snowmen, riding bikes, and beginning
    to shout
Watch me ride, watch me glide, watch me grow…

That which has been is that which will be, and
that which has been done is that which will be
done. So there is nothing new under the sun.
                    —Ecclesiastes 1:9, NASB

Outsourcing

It was 2003/2004, and I was working for a major electronics retail company as their administrator of human resources. The company leadership decided to outsource payroll, benefits, data administration, compensation, payroll taxes, and call center to another company located in Charlotte, North Carolina, with most of the work being sent to Mumbai, India.

This decision made me so angry, and I was not the easiest person to work with and did not care to speak to or associate with the people from India. I could tell the work being transitioned was wrong and voiced my concerns loudly. At one point, the project manager went to my boss and stated I was an "obstructionist" to the contract. When I spoke to my boss, I told him my concerns, and he agreed with me and started attending the meetings, supporting my concerns.

On April 1, 2004, the processes were outsourced. When the first payroll came, there were many errors that I was almost happy in the fact it was failing. Then I got myself together and volunteered to help the outsourcing company and wanted to ensure everyone got paid correctly.

During this time, I would travel to the outsourcer's office and would fly there. On one trip, I boarded the plane and went to my assigned seat. When I arrived at my seat, laying in it was a Billy Graham pamphlet. I always respected Billy Graham, so I started reading it. The pamphlet was about India and the people who lived there. Funny, I never thought of them as God's people. The pamphlet went on to say that India was different than the other countries. The Billy Graham missionary team visited and worked and saw people in India who accepted Christ as their savior and wanted to start their own churches, witness and ordain their ministers, unlike a lot of countries that always expect the missionaries to stay.

I looked out the plane's window with tears in my eyes. I attended the meetings and went back to my home a few days later. Billy Graham's pamphlet never left my thoughts, and I can certainly say I was being convicted by the Holy Spirit to get my act together. I started praying, crying, and asked for help to change my attitude toward the project and the people from India.

When I went back to work, I walked into my boss' office and told him this story. We both cried and decided to help and teach the people from India instead of not supporting them. This turned everything around. I was given the lead and started meeting with them, teaching them, and getting to know them as people. This time is not my proudest moments, but God forgave me and provided me a great learning.

To complete the story, I worked with the people from India for many years. I learned that many were Christian, and one girl's brother was a pastor in one of Billy Graham's churches they built.

One of the guys from India became a great friend to me and my family. As a matter of fact, I had the pleasure of introducing him to Jesus. A few years later, he thanked me for him getting to know Jesus and his new life. What an opportunity I would have missed if God hadn't stepped in and I listened.

Thank you, Jesus!

Jesus said: "When the spirit of truth
comes, he will guide you into all truth."
—John 16:13, NLT

Respect everyone, and love the family of
believers. Fear God and respect the King.
—1 Peter 2:17, NLT

Too Quick to Judge— Finding Fault in Others

I thank God daily for allowing me to live and watch my family grow and to help them through life's day to day challenges—telling them to not worry about anything, pray about everything (Phil. 4:6).

As we go through storms or challenges, it seems we learn so much from them. After we reflect on challenges, we sometimes remember judging others for actions we did not understand to having to live through our own judgements. I have always said prejudice is nothing more than not understanding others walks. I want to share a few of these learnings I have personally experienced.

- *Rape victims*—early in life, I was so "close" to God, I thought I could not do wrong. One of my sayings was, "A woman cannot be raped, it's like putting a finger in a coke bottle you move it, it cannot go in." I said this until I was raped, and when a large man is on you, the "coke bottle" can't be moved! A hard lesson learned.
- *Crying children*—Why can't people control their children? How many times did I judge someone for not having control of their kids and even yelling at them? Until I had nieces, nephews, children, and grandchildren. They screamed in grocery stores, cried loud in church, disrupted meals in restaurants, crying on planes, etc. After living through all these, I now help those parents/grandparents

with their children/grandchildren. What an understanding I received.

- *Organic food*—I'm not buying organic; children can eat what we eat. *Waste of money*, I said. God gave me a grandson who has a food dye allergy. Do you realize how many items from food, drinks, to toothpaste, medicine have dye? Too many to list. We only buy organic or natural now. We shop at specialized stores where all items are pure. God created us, and we were given the ability to digest real food, not artificial. Our bodies are the same as when He made us— do not harm—no artificial ingredients. We all feel better.
- *Gluten free*—Another trend I said—wrong, my colon may be rejecting gluten. Not a trend but real. I read all labels now.

Too many more life lessons to tell. Thanking God daily for letting me learn these valuable life lessons. We all need to think more about other's needs; walk a mile in their shoes before we judge or be critical of others. Thank you, God, for helping me get the log out of my eye.

> Do not judge so that you will not be judged.
> For in the way you judge, you will be judged
> or by our standard of measure; it will be
> measured to you. Why do you look at the
> speck that is in your brother's eye but do
> not notice the log that is in your own eye?
> —Matthew 7:1–3, NASB

Our Aquarium

As I was sitting in our "piano room" after reading the Bible and finishing a devotional, I asked God what my next devotional could be. Like a brick, I looked at our aquarium, and as I watched the fish, this devotion/story came to me.

Our aquarium has about fifteen fish. They are mostly glow fish except for some algae eaters. All different colors—yellow, blue, orange, purple, white, striped, multicolored, and gray. They all swim together and share the thirty-gallon tank with no issues.

What came to mind were these fish, though different colors, all live together peacefully. However, they *are* "like" fish. How can we then expect humans of all colors to live together in harmony if they are not "like" humans? Evil resides with evil. Christians reside with Christians. Evil wants to destroy Christians, and Christians want to destroy evil. Even though their ways are different—prayer vs murder—goal is the same. The only way and time for humans to live together in peace is when Jesus comes back to gather the saved home and throws the evil leader—devil—into the gates of hell (Rev. 20:10).

Will you go the way of Satan or will you follow Jesus? Truth—if your name is not written in the book of life, you will be thrown into the lake of fire (Rev. 20:15).

I think of my family, friends, people I know of that don't know—all will be cast into the Lake of Fire with no second chance. My prayer and hope are that all receive Jesus as their personal savior and get their names written in the book of life. I need to take a more active role in telling and showing others the way of salvation. Thank you for this opportunity—my Jesus, my Savior, and my redeemer. Amen!

Thank you, God, for my salvation. Looking forward to spending eternity with you and all the saved! Amen!

Recommend the reading of Revelation 20 and 21

> Beloved, now we are children of God, and it
> has not appeared as yet what we will be. We
> know that when He appears, we will be like
> Him, because we will see Him just as He is.
> —1 John 3:2, NASB

> Do not be deceived, God is not mocked; for
> whatever a man sows, this he will also reap.
> —Galatians 6:7, NASB

Challenges

It is almost 2:00 a.m., and my current challenge is not being able to sleep. A lot on my mind.

Life has been full of challenges, successes, and of course, failures. Growing up, I was tall and skinny. I became the class clown to hide a lot of feelings from me being called skinny jokes. Funny, now I am overweight, and no one would ever believe I suffered from skinny jokes. I think I shut a lot of people out as I've learned later in life that my classmates thought me standoffish. Funny, I succeeded during these years though.

After school, life continued to be full of goals and my challenges to reach them. I made mistakes but kept on going.

Now later in life and writing about these challenges, I realize how small they were and really didn't matter. So small I don't even care to go in depth as I write. However, each one made me whom I am today. As you travel the road called life—never give up, depend on God, and you will get through them all.

> I thank my God always concerning you for the
> grace of God which was given you in Christ
> Jesus, that in everything you were enriched
> in Him, in all speech and all knowledge,
> even as the testimony concerning Christ was
> confirmed in you, so that you are not lacking
> in any gift, awaiting eagerly the revelation of

our Lord Jesus Christ, who will also confirm
you to the end, blameless in the day of our
Lord Jesus Christ. God is faithful, through
whom you were called into fellowship
with His Son, Jesus Christ our Lord.
—1 Corinthians 1:4–9, NASB

Alaska—God's Creation Untouched by Man

I was able to mark Alaska off my bucket list after many years. I do not really know what drew me there. I had heard of the beauty, but nothing prepared me for the sights.

Everywhere we traveled, we saw beauty. The highlight was Denali National Park. Millions of acres untouched by man. Every time I saw something, I thought, how beautiful. Then I would see another mountain, another field, another stream, and it was more beautiful than the last. I felt closer to God and his beautiful creations than I ever have before. A trip worth it all. I think this is how heaven is going to be. We will praise God, see the glory, turn around, see more beauty, and praise Him louder. Such a great God we serve here, and we get to serve Him throughout eternity. Thank you, Jesus!

> Since you have been raised to new life with Christ, set your sights on the realities of heaven, where Christ sits in the place of honor at God's right hand. Think about the things of Heaven, not the things of earth. For you died to this life and your real life is hidden with Christ in God. And when Christ, who is your life, is revealed to the whole world, you will share in all his glory.
> —Colossians 3:1–4, NLT

Armor of God—My Granddaughter, Addie

One of the Bible lessons we teach our children is the armor of God.

Recently, our granddaughter was visiting, and we all attended Church. She went to Children's Church where they were beginning to learn the "armor of God." The teacher stated that at the end, each child would be tested on it. This was the first day. Not sure how it happened, but the teacher "tested" our granddaughter that day. The next week at church, the teacher brought me Addie's certificate where she had passed the quiz, and she knew the armor of God.

A couple of weeks later, Addie and her parents came to visit. I gave her the certificate and stuffed animal the Children's Church teacher had given me for her.

I told Addie how proud we were of her, and I asked, "Did you learn that in your Sunday school?"

She said a matter-of-factly, "No, I learned it when I was reading the Bible one day!"

I do not think my heart has ever been so pleased. To know that my granddaughter on her own was reading, studying, and remembering God's Word. Thanks to her parents for making sure she attends church, and thanks to God for opening her heart to His truth.

Never underestimate your children. Addie is now eleven years old, and I know she will continue in her walk with God and will always wear the armor of God.

I have no greater joy than this, to hear
of my children walking in the truth.
—3 John 4, NASB

Grandchildren are the crowning glory of the
aged; parents are the pride of their children.
—Proverbs 17:6, NLT

Direct your children onto the right path, and
when they are older, they will not leave it.
—Proverbs 22:6, NLT

Put on the full armor of God, so
that you will be able to stand firm
against the schemes of the devil.
—Ephesians 6:11, NASB

Journey to Salvation— My Cousin Becky

One of my many life's blessings were my aunts and uncles. One aunt was always a favorite and never stopped making us laugh. After ten years of marriage, my aunt and uncle had a daughter and named her Rebecca (Becky her nickname). Becky and I became closer when we grew older even though we were many years apart in age.

After her parents passing and when my parents passed, we once again connected. I can thank Facebook for that.

One time while visiting my Aunt Jenny, several of my cousins came up to her house to visit. We sat around the table, ate, laughed, remembering old times, and cried. During this time, the subject of being saved came up. We knew Becky had not taken that step and talked with her and wept. Becky kept saying I have too many sins, etc. Even though we shared our stories of salvation, she just turned her head.

As we continued to visit, the day wore on. My other cousins left. When Becky got up to leave, I walked her to the door, she started crying. She said to me, "I know I need to accept Jesus, I'm just afraid I cannot live right." I hugged her and told her I would send her some information and pray for her daily. My heart cried as I felt I had let Becky down and most of all God.

As the years passed, I sent Becky cards, called her, sent her pamphlets. She never made that decision. Another time when I once again was visiting my Aunt Jenny who was now sick with cancer, my cousin, Barbara, and I met Becky for lunch. We were both so happy to see her. We ate, laughed, and prayed. This would be the last time I saw Becky alive that I would consider quality time. I saw her for a brief moment at my Cousin Connie's wake. Strange how things work. My aunt had died in October; and my cousin, Connie, who had fixed our lunches the day we all visited Aunt Jenny, died two months later.

Shortly after, Becky got sick. She had been ill for some time but refused to see a doctor. One night, she was taken to the hospital, and it was discovered she had colon cancer.

I called her, sent her cards and flowers with a burden on my heart for her salvation. My cousins, Justin and Courtney (Aunt Jenny's grandson), were burdened as well. Justin would call and go see her and pray with her. I prayed with her on the phone and kept sending her cards, etc.

One day, Justin called me and said Becky had called him and wanted to be saved. He read the Bible Scriptures to her and prayed the prayer of salvation. I can still remember my overflowing joy and peace celebrating her victory in Jesus.

Then one day, my phone rang, and it was Becky. She was crying. I asked her what was wrong, and she apologized to me that she had called Justin instead of me to be saved. I could not believe it. I immediately told her that it was not mine to do. That God had led her to Justin and that no one can pray like him. We then spent time rejoicing in her victory and in her regrets that she had not taken the salvation step sooner. I advised her to stop thinking that way so she would not lose her joy.

I thanked God for her salvation Not long after our conversation, Becky died. Even though she succumbed to her illnesses, we all had peace in our hearts that the angels took her to heaven where she is reunited with her parents for all eternity. I'll see them again someday. Glad she didn't wait too long!

> For He says, "At the acceptable time I listened to you, and on the day of salvation I helped you." Behold now is "the acceptable time," behold, now is "the day of Salvation." (2 Cor. 6:2, NASB)

Do not put off your decision to accept God's offer of Salvation.

Born of the Spirit— My Grandson, William

In a snap of a finger, a blink of an eye, or in this case, a phone call, your life forever changes. One day, as I was at the airport getting ready to board the plane for home, my phone rang. It was my daughter, who was not married, and she went on to tell me she was pregnant. I was in shock to say the least. *Another storm*, I thought. I knew her boyfriend but did not think they were that serious. I told her I was boarding the plane, and we would talk when I arrived home but not to worry, we would get through this together. It was a three-and-a-half-hour flight. I prayed and cried all the way home and knew somehow this would be ok.

Nine months later, she gave birth to a little boy. My other daughter and I were at his birth. Immediately after his birth, the respiratory team was there and took him as he was not breathing or crying. My daughter and I sat down and prayed. In a few seconds that seemed an eternity, he started to cry, and his skin turned a beautiful pink. I knew then he was touched by God.

Her little boy, my grandson, has become one of the most outgoing, loving, and caring child of God. He suffers from severe hemophilia A, with an inhibitor, the rarest kind. He has had a port since he was one year old in order to get his infusions. He went for many years getting daily infusions of Factor VIII to stop any bleeds but developed an inhibitor that was "eating" the factor and his B cells, causing other health issues for him. This never quenched his spirit. As a matter of fact, his illness has only provided him and us opportunities to witness for God. He had spontaneous bleeds two to three times a month for several years. In December 2017, a miracle drug, HemLibra, was put on the market; and he started receiving weekly shots. As miracles go, he has not had a spontaneous bleed since then and only had to take bleed infusions once due to a tooth coming in which caused bleeds.

When he had just turned six years, he accepted Jesus as his personal savior and was baptized. He is a second grader now, enjoying his second grade. Throughout his short life, he has been given the opportunity to meet people in many hospitals and treatment centers. Everyone we meet always tells us the same thing; he is a little evangelist.

Our grandson lives his faith daily, which at times is larger than life. He had led a toy drive from church for St. Jude Affiliate in Charlotte, of which he is a patient. He has sung solos and duets with his Mom in church, performed in a musical at his school, and lead prayers without hesitation at home, church, the hospital, or wherever he sees the need.

Recently, he was invited to a law firm in Charlotte that had raised money for his 5K hemophilia walk team—Will Power. I took him to their office to pick up the donations and to say thanks.

On the way to the office, we passed a homeless man. As we walked on and entered the building, he turned to me and said, "I am sad." I asked why and he said matter of fact—"we didn't give anything to the homeless man." I said we would do it on our way out, which I must confess, I forgot in an instant as I was focusing on other things.

At the continental breakfast, he gave a speech of thanks, talked to everyone, made new friends, and then visited each office to distribute their staff appreciation gifts. I stayed in the conference room as he walked around with the firm's marketing director, approximately twenty minutes.

When they returned to the room, he went to the muffins and started packing them up. I reprimanded him for being greedy and asked that he leave the muffins for the staff members that he didn't need them. He said, "I'm getting these for the homeless man." God then reprimanded me. The marketing director got a bag and helped him fill it with yogurt, larger muffins, too. My grandson got napkins and several spoons in case the homeless man wanted to share.

We left with him carefully, carrying the bag of food. We walked out of the building, and the homeless man was still there. My grandson let go of my hand and ran to him, saying, "This is for you." The man looked at this little boy with love and said, "God bless you." My grandson said immediately, "God blesses you." The man cried, and so did I. My grandson put the blesses in present tense. We walked on, and I told my grandson that he did what Jesus would have done. We looked back, and the man was going through the bag of food ever so gently. On the way to the car, my grandson said that when he got home, he was going to get in his piggy bank and bring him some money. The lady at the firm had told us that the man was there most every day and that he was nice. I promised my grandson we would go back and visit him again and take him other things.

> But Jesus said, "Let the children alone, and do
> not hinder them from coming to Me; for the
> kingdom of heaven belongs to such as these."
> —Matthew 19:14, NASB

> For I was hungry and you gave me nothing
> to eat; I was thirsty, and you gave Me nothing
> to drink; I was a stranger, and you did not
> invite Me in; naked, and you did not clothe
> Me; sick, and in prison, and you did not visit
> Me.' "Then they themselves also will answer,
> 'Lord, when did we see you hungry or thirsty,
> or a stranger, or naked, or sick, or in prison,
> and did not take care of You?' "Then He
> will answer them, 'Truly I say to you, to the
> extent that you did not do it to one of the
> least of these, you did not do it to Me.'"
> —Mathew 25:42–45, NASB

trusting…

End of High School—A New Journey

How fast does life change! On May 30, 1967, I graduated from high school in a small town in West Virginia. I had been accepted to attend West Virginia Institute of Technology in Montgomery, West Virginia, and was planning to go at the end of August 1967. During my senior year, I, along with other business students, also took the Civil Service Exam in case we wanted to work for the United States Government in Washington DC. I passed the exam, and since my sister and her husband lived in Virginia not far from DC, I always knew this might be an option. As a matter of fact, I accepted a job with the Department of Agriculture to start September 11, 1967, as college was not firm, and I always believe in a backup.

Mid-August, I knew my parents were struggling with how they were going to pay for my college. My plan was to stay with my aunt and uncle in Montgomery and their son, my cousin, who was going to WV Tech with me. Then, my aunt said I could not stay with them. My cousin and I were hurt. So hurt we both decided not to go to college. I called my contact at the Department of Agriculture and asked if I could start a week early on September 5. My cousin joined the Marines and left shortly for Vietnam. Both our lives changed forever. My cousin and I kept in touch throughout his Vietnam tour. I wrote him daily. He was badly injured and came home never to be the healthy man he was. At our MaMaw's funeral he brought me his Purple Heart Medal. His Dad asked him why he was giving it to me and my cousin told his Dad that my daily letters got him through Vietnam. My cousin and I remained friends until he died.

My Mom and Dad were angry at my aunt but supported me in my decision, but inside, I knew they were relieved. Dad took me to a car lot, and my Dad financed a 1965 White Ford Mustang for me, but Mom and Dad never made a payment as I took it on immediately.

Life was a whirlwind for a few weeks as I got ready to start my career. My parents and I went to visit my sister and her husband. My Dad and by brother-in-law took me to DC to find where I was going to work as I was driving there alone the next day. Washington DC was a huge place, but I was not afraid, only excited.

On September 5, 1967, I drove to my first job, wearing a maroon suit, maroon heels, and carrying a maroon purse, similar to the clothes I had seen women wear on TV. During orientation, I was told I was going to work for the Food Stamp Division in Rosslyn, Virginia. *Where?* The leader found a girl going there to ride with me and show me the way. We got to Rosslyn, walked a mile, and got to our new jobs. Oh, how I remember my feet hurt, I never wore those maroon heels again. I was introduced to everyone, and the branch chief asked me where I lived and how I was getting to work. After I told him, he called a gentleman into his office and asked him if he could make room in his carpool for me. He said yes, and I started riding with them the next day. I rode in this carpool for several years. God took care of me and is still doing so today.

I have reflected on this life change many times. If I had gone to college to become a teacher or if I had started September 11, I was assigned to work in the poultry division—different people, different job, and different life experiences. I have never regretted this journey. Thank God for great parents and for the people He put in my paths to ensure I was always taken care of!

Depend on God daily and through every aspect of your life.

> I will bless the Lord who guides me; even at
> night my heart instructs me. I know the Lord
> is always with me. I will not be shaken, for
> he is right beside me. No wonder my heart is
> glad, and I rejoice. My body rests in safety.
> —Psalm 16:7–9, NLT

Sarah's Affliction and Strength

At eighteen, I went to work, and my first director (boss) had polio, and it affected his right side. I learned to help him put on his coat and little things to make his day better. A few years later, I worked for a member of Congress who had polio, and it affected his left arm. I was comfortable in helping him with his coat and daily things as I had learned that from my first boss.

In 1978, I gave birth to a beautiful baby girl. When she was sixteen months old, the doctors noticed that her right side was developing differently. After many tests, she was diagnosed with having a stroke while I carried her in my pregnancy. It affected her right side. Since God had provided me with these two bosses, I was equipped to help Sarah with her weaker side.

Sarah had her first surgery at three to give her ankle a flex and another surgery due to the stroke between her junior and senior year of school to straighten her leg.

There exists no therapy to teach her how to use her hand. PT/OT works for those who once used their fine motor skills and reteach the brain, but if you never learned it, no therapy exists. So, she had to learn to compensate with her left hand and dominate side.

We gave her ballet to ensure her flex stayed put, and we were surrounded by people who came up with ideas on how to use her hand. She could not cut with scissors as at the time, left-handed scissors did not exist for many in school. We purchased a lot of left-handed scissors for the school as we knew she could not be the only left-handed student there. Her kindergarten teacher had a sister with a hand like Sarah's and gave Sarah a ball to hold to keep her hand open. Sarah had the same teacher in first grade. We always laughed that they got promoted together.

Sarah played French horn—a perfect instrument for a left-hander. Her right side was smaller and shorter, so we came up with creative ways for her success. Putting a block on her bicycle pedal so her right foot could reach it. She learned to play piano with one hand. I could go on and on. It seems each challenge given her, God gave us an idea for her to succeed.

Today, she is forty, and God is still providing ways. She has great doctors and teaches K-4 music. She has been a music director at a church and still sings for God. She is still learning life, and God continues giving her learning opportunities. She had always hated the word, "compensate," because that is what people always told her to do. Instead, she learned to do it her way and not live in a left-handed world, and she thanks God daily for putting her with people to learn and to teach. Sarah's verse she has always lived by, then and today:

> I can do all things through Him who strengthens me. Nevertheless, you have done well to share with me in my affliction!
> —Phil. 4:13–14, NASB

Obedience to God

As far back as I can remember, being obedient, obeying the rules and laws was taught by my parents, grandparents, teachers, church leaders, bosses, etc. Most of these were man-made.

It only came later in life did I understand the importance of obeying God. I have failed God many times. I disobeyed when I was called to a missionary in my early twenties. I disobeyed when I didn't write this book earlier. I'm not talking about sin, I've done that and asked forgiveness, but not trusting Him as He was leading me, I regret. What did He have in store for me? What blessings have I missed? Once I learned to be obedient, life, even with its storms, has been better. I learned that if you pray about it and listen, He will show you the way. If you feel you need to do something and don't, you may not be obedient to God's wishes.

During the past several months, God has been calling me to do something else—to go and worship someplace else. I loved my church, but I know that I have fulfilled my mission there, and now I am on a new journey to serve Him where he sends me.

After a conversation with my family, it seems we have all been feeling the same. God is sending us as a unit. We have decided to follow Him and let Him lead us to our next place of service for Him. It may be we all need to be fed and revitalized in order to serve Him. We will be fed by reading our Bibles, hearing His word preached and most of all our prayers, and open Hearts to hear His call. We are excited for our next worship experience. God, watch over us, lead us in the right path. and "kick" us if we falter. We listened and God led us to a new place of worship that has been praying for a family with our spiritual gifts. God is so good. Thanks to God for His love and leadership. I will obey your call. Amen.

> But Samuel replied (to Saul) What is more
> pleasing to the Lord; your burnt offerings
> and sacrifices or your obedience to His voice?
> Listen! Obedience is better than sacrifice,
> and submission is better than offering the fat
> of rams. Rebellion is as sinful as witchcraft,
> and stubbornness as bad as worshiping idols.
> So, because you have rejected the command
> of the Lord, he has rejected you as king.
> —1 Samuel 15:22–23, NLT

Vultures

One day, my husband and I were driving from town, and on the side of the road were two vultures, eating an animal—too far gone to recognize. In the air a couple miles down the road, vultures were flying above in their circle, surrounding their next meal, which we saw was a fallen deer that the vultures were preparing to devour. As we rode on, we talked about how God created everything for a purpose. Most animals would get ill, eating decaying rotten meat. However, the vultures survive on it. That is their purpose, to clear the land. God thought of everything. It caused us to pause and think—what is our purpose, and are we doing it? What is man's purpose?

The world has moved a long way from God's purpose. However, I can pray for mankind, but I must recognize to do what God has called me to do. I'm behind on that. Writing this book is one I need to finish and publish. I've been writing since 2002 and still not finished with thirty-five reflections. Shame on *me*! I've asked God to forgive my slothfulness and will move forward full force now.

How about you? Are you delaying what God has called you to do? Have you mediated on His word to discover what His will for you is? Take the time and search for His desire for your life. I know I'll have to give an accounting to Him—I need to stay the course, so He can give me other things to do for His kingdom! How about you?

> For God is not unjust so as to forget your work
> and the love which you have shown toward

His name, in having ministered and in still
ministering to the Saints. And we desire that
each one of you show the same diligence so
as to realize the full assurance of hope until
the end, so that you will not be sluggish, but
imitators of those who through faith and
patience inherit the promises. For when God
made the promise to Abraham, since He could
swear by no one greater, He swore by Himself.
—Hebrews 6:10–13, NASB

Just as the gathering of vultures shows
there is a carcass nearby, so these
signs indicate the end is near.
—Matthew 24:28, NLT

In God's Time

Everyday, we ask for things we need from God. Usually, we feel these are needed now. My mind is bringing forth many things that went "right" because we waited on God's time. My husband and I believe that if it comes easy, it's God's plan, and if it has obstacles, we stop the pursuit. I'm not saying don't work toward a goal, I'm saying do everything and pray that everything happens on God's timetable. He is in control.

To illustrate a few life examples:

- *My grandniece, Julia's, heart transplant.* At the time, it seemed we were losing her—but on time, she got her heart, and it never has had one rejection. We celebrated ten years without rejection March 2019.
- *College loans.* We tried to get a college loan for our daughter to attend a Christian college. We struggled, and it finally came through. Turns out the loan was awful and so was that university. We came home after several weeks, continued, and succeeded in her education and got future loans with no problems.
- *Buying cars.* If we experience a hard time at the dealership, we walk away. I had a sort of easy time with my last car but had to put more dollars down than I wanted. I should have listened to the Holy Spirit and walked away. The car is great, but the payments are higher than I should

have accepted, and each month, I struggle with them and praying for a way out.

- *Our church's pastor.* As chairman of the selection committee, we prayed for God's guidance and strength. Many church members were pushing for someone as it would have been easy. That was not the right leader, we waited, we listened, we even changed our rules, and God provided us with a great pastor; and the church has grown in love, spirit, and salvations. Thank you, Jesus.
- *Marriage.* I had a list of qualities I wanted in a husband and patiently waited. Even though my friends got married, and my minister tried to get me to marry another man saying that my "list' was not reasonable. I met my husband, and before we married, I was in the hospital, he was there, and that minister came to visit, I was happy to introduce him as the man who completed the list. Even he had to admit I was right in waiting.

I could go on and on but those few came to mind. Just listen, as for God's guidance and your patience, and even though there will be storms, there are always God's reasons. Trust Him alone! Take time to reflect on the times you made your timetable without God and the times you depended and waited upon Him—In His Time.

Wait patiently for the Lord. Be brave and
courageous. Yes, wait patiently for the Lord.
—Psalm 27:14, NLT

Family

Family has been, is, and will always be important. I was fortunate to be born to a loving Father and Mother. Even though their childhoods were difficult, they provided unconditional love and a nice home with very little means. I had a sister and brother. I also had many aunts, uncles, cousins, and wonderful grandparents. Even though my PaPaw Hall (my Dad's father) died when I was four, I learned of him from both my Mom and Dad. I grew up with my other three grandparents whom I loved and learned from them.

Our family grew when my sister married her husband, Lloyd. He became a very loving brother-in-law who welcomed me in their home to live when I graduated from high school in 1967. I lived with them until I was twenty-one. In later 1969, I wanted a new car. I found a Chevrolet Monte Carlo—1970 model, the first year they made them. I needed a thousand dollars for a down payment. Without hesitation, Lloyd gave me the money for the car with no mention of me having to pay it back. He also took care of my cars, changing the oil, fixing them if they broke, and was a great friend even though we sometimes argued like family. He never asked for the money back even though I paid it back over time.

Since then, our family grew with my husband and our children, my sister's children, my brother, his wife and son, and then my nieces and nephews and their families. We will continue to grow as a family.

My heart yearns that everyone in my family become members of God's family by accepting Jesus as their personal savior, which is the only thing that matters in life. Lloyd gave me money and a place to live, and my parents giving me a good home—all goes away. Salvation is the only real thing.

There was a time when my sister's children and my children were growing up that we would go to the beach each summer. We'd play in the ocean, eat great meals, argue, make-up, and start over. One summer after my sister's oldest child finished a year of college, we once again went to the beach. One of her college classmates brought her cousin to spend the day with us. As life goes, her cousin and my niece fell in love and married a few years later. This was over thirty years ago.

During these years, I grew to love him as my nephew. He has a gentle soul. I pray for him and all my sister's family. I am not sure if all my family, including my cousins, have accepted Jesus as their personal savior. Even though they are nice people, I'm not sure of their relationship with God. Where will they spend eternity?

Many of my family have been saved and are living for God. Many have not and those are the ones I pray to know Jesus. I pray for those who are living for Him and thank God they made the choice. However, my deepest concern is for the unsaved. I feel it is up to me to tell them or I'll lose favor with God as I think some do not know the way to salvation. I, as a Christian, must tell others about His love and heaven.

My brother-in-law, Lloyd, passed away unexpectedly March 16, 2019. I know he was saved, and he was the rock of his family. One of his daughters found his Bible after his death, and throughout it, there were texts underlined as he read and studied. His death gave us the opportunity to reflect on Jesus and his wonderful saving grace. I will write the rest of this story at another time. But in the meantime, I will continue to pray for all my family and friends as they are a burden on my heart, and I must follow through on God's command.

> Jesus replied, "I tell you the truth, unless you
> are born again, you cannot see the Kingdom
> of God." "What do you mean?" exclaimed

Nicodemus. "How can an old man go back into his mother's womb and be born again?" Jesus replied, "I assure you; no one can enter the Kingdom of God without being born of water and the Spirit. Humans can reproduce only human life, but the Holy Spirit gives birth to spiritual life. So don't be surprised when I say, 'you must be born again.' The wind blows wherever it wants. Just as you can hear the wind but can't tell where it comes from or where it is going, so you can't explain how people are born of the spirit."
—John 3:3–8, NLT

Make it your goal to live a quiet life, minding your own business and working with your hands just as we instructed you before. Then people who are not believers will respect the way you live, and you will not need to depend on others.
—1 Thessalonians 4:11–12, NLT

Trusting God and His Spiritual Gifts—My Daughter, Beverly

God has been so wonderful to our family. He has given so many varied talents throughout our generations. Music always surrounded our lives through my Mom, my grandparents, and many uncles and aunts from both sides of our family. Leadership is one of our spiritual gifts and has been evident throughout. Caring and love for others is also very prevalent. Artistic talent exists from generation to generation. Carvings, paintings, storytelling, crafts, and other tangible expressions of art prevail. Our youngest daughter was given all the talents listed. She can sing, play musical instruments, and can draft and paint as well as being a leader in her career and family. She is a very caring person and her artwork, jewelry-making, and anything she wants to make is beautiful. She is also a child of God and never hesitates to tell or show others how God plays a role in all things.

My husband and I early on knew that the most important thing we could do in life is to ensure we taught our children about God and His salvation plan through Jesus Christ. We also knew we would support them in their talents and the path they chose, praying they would do what they love and never stop worshiping God. Our daughter at times does not feel her art is good enough, her singing is of par, and she questions other talents, even though God has provided her so many spiritual gifts. However, she continues to move forward and grow in all areas of her life. She leaves her concerns to God and waits on Him, then always moves in the right direction with good results. Sometimes, we want her to move faster, but she waits on God, and it turns out successful. We then thank her for her faith and her talents increase and get better each year.

We all need to pause and take this life lesson from her. Let's not rush to judgment or give up—keep on and never stop trusting God. Thank you, Beverly, for your dedication and love. Enjoy the art room, your family, your job, your church, and all the things God is providing for you. Keep up the faith.

> For through the law I died to the Law, so that
> I might live to God. I have been crucified with
> Christ; and it is no longer I who live, but Christ
> lives in me; and the life which I now live in
> the flesh, I live by faith in the Son of God,
> who loved me and gave Himself up for me.
> —Galatians 2:19–20, NASB

Trusting God Throughout Life's Tragedies—My MaMaw Hall

No one understands or knows why some people seem to have or go through more sorrow than others. The saying, "What does not kill you makes you stronger," could have been written for my paternal grandmother.

Throughout her life, she suffered many tragedies. She had nine children—my Dad, Paul; his brothers, Fred, Donald, Willard, and Oria; his sisters Elitha, Tennia Mae, Ruby, and Betty and then loved another and adopted him, Teddy.

When Ruby was six years and Oria was just a little older, he got a gun and shot Ruby accidently, and she died. When Oria was a teenager, he was riding on logs in the back of a logging truck, the logs came loose, rolled off the truck, crushed him, and he died. PaPaw Hall died at age fifty-nine from black lung. Her son, Willard, died at thirty-nine from cirrhosis of the liver caused by alcohol. Her adopted son, Teddy, died in a car wreck in his early thirties caused by a drunken driver. Her son, Fred, suffered severe injuries in an alcohol caused car wreck, he was drunk in that car. He was in the hospital for almost a year and suffered throughout his life. (Fred got saved later in life and spent decades singing and playing instruments for God.) Her son, Donald, died of colon cancer in his fifties. Her daughter, Elitha, died of cancer. Her daughter, Tennia Mae, died of colon/brain cancer. Her daughter, Betty, died from a gunshot wound. The only children to survive her was my Dad and my Uncle Fred.

She lived through all of these personal tragedies and never lost her humor. She had other tragedies from her sons/daughter-in laws, but these were her children I mentioned.

Throughout her life, she depended on Jesus, and later, she and my Uncle Donald lived together and worshiped God together.

She was ninety-four when she went to her reward. But during my life with her, I saw her strength and positive outlook on life. I have shared her life story many times as her never-ending love of God, her humor, her love, and her love of life has only inspired and made me stronger as I face trials and hurts during mine.

I am glad she was my MaMaw and look forward to seeing her again. She always depended on God to help her through these trials and often told us to let God's will be done.

> Then Jesus said, "come to me, all of you who
> are weary and carry heavy burdens, and I
> will give you rest. Take my yoke upon you.
> Let me teach you, because I am humble
> and gentle at heart, and you will find rest
> for your souls. For my yoke is easy to bear,
> and the burden I give you is light."
> —Matthew 11:28–30, NLT

A Few of Life's Choices

Life is filled with choices. Even when we don't choose, we make a choice. In sixth grade, we always chose our teachers by going to their room on the first day of school. I went to Mrs. Hale's room as she was known to be the best teacher. It was so crowded the principal asked for volunteers to go to other six grade teachers. I left voluntarily and went to Mr. Halsey's class, had a great year and made life long friends. Mrs. Hale, whose husband worked with my Dad, stopped by my Dad's office and asked why I had moved. Dad liked Mr. Halsey and said I could stay in his class. Later in life, I learned that in our small town, students that were in Mrs. Hale's class were considered smarter than others. This affected me throughout my school years as I was never put in the "first" homeroom even though I excelled in school and was inducted into the honor society.

My next choice was college. I was accepted at West Virginia Institute of Technology and was college bound until my aunt who lived blocks from the college told my parents I couldn't stay with them. I then went to work in DC, and my cousin, my aunt's son, chose to go to Vietnam as he was not happy that we could not go to college together.

My next choice was starting a week earlier in DC. If I had kept my first week, I would have worked in the poultry department at agriculture instead of food and nutrition services. I love chickens.

I was given the opportunity to be a missionary in Australia but did not take the opportunity as I did not want to be gone from my family for three years. A choice I have always regretted.

I could go on and on with my life choices and how each affected me. All of the ones I have mentioned occurred before I was twenty.

After my children were born, I taught them about choices and relayed my life stories. I bought them stones with the word, "choices," on it and told them to carry it in their pockets and hold onto and think when they were about to make a choice, hoping they would make the right one.

The choice I made at nine years old that has impacted my life and those around me was when I chose to stay after church one Sunday night and accepted Jesus as my personal savior. That choice changed my life and was before my sixth grade choice of classrooms.

I remember leaving Mrs. Hale's class because I felt for the teachers that needed students. I chose Mr. Halsey as his room was in the basement, and I thought it cool to have a male teacher. I chose not to go to college as I was hurt and angry at my aunt. I'm not sure I forgave her, and she has passed. My cousin and I remained friends until his death. He gave me his Purple Heart he earned in Vietnam as he said my letters got him through the war.

I've had a great career, so the choice I made about work was a good one. My choice about serving God is still my most important, and I thank God daily for loving me and for his son, Jesus, and my salvation! Choose salvation today.

> And working together with Him, we also
> urge you not to receive the grace of God in
> vain…for He says, "At the acceptable time I
> listened to you, and on the day of salvation I
> helped you." Behold, now is "the acceptable
> time," behold now is "The day of Salvation."
> —2 Corinthians 6:1–2, NASB

Be Aware of Idols

My stepdaughter posted on Facebook a picture of four rosaries given to her by different Catholic family members. She was raised in a Catholic church until she was fourteen when she came to live with us. She accepted Jesus as her savior and was baptized while serving the Air Force. She is in church today, and both her sons have accepted Jesus as their savior.

When she posted the picture of the four rosaries, asking how best to display them and that she had carried them with her throughout all her moves, I cautioned her in having idols. Many people will not remove a cross necklace as it makes them feel closer to God. I used to do that. Others display crosses, Bibles, etc., throughout their house and dusting them with care. It is all good to have these items or others that you like. The harm is when we think upon these objects as items with power and look to them instead of God.

God is not in those idols—anything that you depend on, look upon, care about as something that will keep you from harm, is making that item an idol. Therefore, be careful in your worship. Depend on God, who has sent Jesus to die for our sins and once saved sends the Holy Spirit to dwell inside of us and not some inanimate object will keep you on the right path.

I used to make sure I carried the Bible with me for protection, that was wrong. The Bible is our helper when we read/study and let God talk to us through His word. Just carrying it and never opening it does nothing for us at all. Just be careful to only trust God!

Then God spoke all these words, saying, I am the Lord your God, who brought you out of the land of Egypt, out of the house of slavery. You shall have no other gods before Me. You shall not make for yourself an idol, or any likeness of what is in heaven above on the earth beneath or in the water under the earth. You shall not worship them or serve them; for I, the LORD your God, am a jealous God, visiting the iniquity of the fathers on the children, on the third and the fourth generations of these who hate Me, but showing lovingkindness to thousands, to those who love Me and keep my commandments."

—Exodus 20:1–6, NASB

(Jesus Speaking) "If you keep My commandments, you will abide in My love; just as I have kept My Father's commandments and abide in His love. These things I have spoken to you so that My joy may be in you, and that your joy may be made full. This is My commandment, that you love one another, as I have loved you."

—John 15:10–12, NASB

The End

Blessed be the name of the Lord from this time forth and forever. —Psalm 113-2, NASB

About the Author

Linda Lou Hall Hodges accepted Jesus Christ as her savior at nine years of age in a small church in a small town in West Virginia. After graduating high school, she left West Virginia and worked her way up from a Clerk-Steno with the United States Government to managing two congressional offices. After leaving the government, she worked in private industry retiring from a Fortune 500 company as an executive. She served in public office as a school board member/chairman and has served in many churches as their choir director and pianist. She is currently the founder and owner of Keyrock Women's Ministries where she serves as a life coach, mentor, teacher, and encourager to women, young and aged.

Her career has enabled her to live a diverse life, traveling the globe, including all US states except four. Her experiences brought her in touch with many different people and experiencing different cultures that enabled her to gain valuable life experiences that she shares with the reader. Throughout her life's journey, she always came back to her foundation in Christ to help her through the bad times and to recognize the good times.

Linda has been married to her husband for forty-three years. She has two daughters, two stepdaughters, and four grandchildren. She retired with over fifty years of experience, most of which was in human resources. Her husband is retired from the United States Air Force.

CPSIA information can be obtained
at www.ICGtesting.com
Printed in the USA
BVHW092000030120
568542BV00003B/34/P